GUARDIAN CAR BUYER SERVICE INC.

INSIDE SECRETS OF
AUTO DEALERS

BY

DAVID E. NORDSTROM

PUBLISHED BY GUARDIAN CAR BUYER SERVICE, INC.

Published by

Guardian Car Buyer Service
P.O Box 1633
Riverside, CA 92502-1633

Edited by: Robert Wulf

Manufactured in the United States Of America thru:

Asia Print Ltd.
26522 La Alameda Suite 275,
Mission Viejo, CA 92691

Cover © 1995 Guardian Car Buyer Service

Cover design by: Design Service, Fullerton CA

Produced by: Capital Communications, Irvine, CA

ISBN: 0-9640360-2-9

Library Of Congress Catalog Card Number: 95-094548

If your local U.S. bookstore is out of stock, copies of this book may be obtained by mailing check or money order for $12.95 per book (plus $2.50 to cover postage and handling) to: Guardian Car Buyer Service; P.O. Box 1633; Riverside CA 92502-1633

Revised Edition.

Dedicated to:

NANCY C. JOHNSON

ACKNOWLEDGMENTS

I would like to thank all of the individuals inside and outside the auto industry for their support and assistance while researching this book. Without their effort the book could not have been possible. I would especially like to thank my Father, Floyd Nordstrom, who gave me my first break in the auto business as well as instilling in me the belief that honesty is always the best policy regardless of the profession.

I would also like to thank the following people for all of their support and encouragement when I needed it most: Paul and Nancy Johnson, Charles Wanta and Family, Timothy Haase, and Sandra Bascom-Haase.

And finally, I would like to thank the many participants in the City of Grand Terrace who generously acted as test marketers to help confirmed the accuracy of the book.

FOREWORD

This book is the result of a long and difficult struggle by a dedicated group of individuals inside the auto industry whose efforts culminate the art of purchasing a new or used automobile in America today. It is a portrayal of first hand experiences of those individuals who utilize the many deceptive trade practices and policies used by new and used car dealerships to further enhance their own prosperity. This book attempts to increase buyer awareness by educating all consumers with the necessary information needed to win at the art of car buying.

To get the very most out of this text, we suggest before entering the market, you read the book in its entirety. It has been proven, individuals who read the book first, have better results with the final outcome of their transaction than those who simply scan the text looking for pointers. This is the best way to utilize the material.

By carefully following the instructions in this book, step by step, you will save a significant amount of money and needless aggravation. Though we have tried to cover all of the important facts regarding the automotive industry, there is no substitute for good old fashion common sense. The one rule that seems to work best when dealing with the wily beast known as the "car salesman," is to establish early on that you are commanding the negotiation and you have the power to say no.

It is the car salesperson's job to get you emotionally involved and committed to a deal as soon as possible. Your best defense is to stay uncommitted, time is on your side. Do not allow the salesperson to manipulate you into making a decisions you're not ready to make. The best way to do this is to simply state you are not ready to make a decision or leave the dealership with a friendly salutation and go to another.

Remember, the salesperson has a vested interest in selling you a car. He wants you to buy a car from him a lot more than you do. Your interest lies it getting the best deal you can, no matter who the salesperson or dealership. If you are truly getting the best deal they have to offer, it will be the same deal 24 hours later. Otherwise, you can be assured a better deal exists, there or somewhere else.

My goal, when writing this book was to provide the consumer with one of the most comprehensive and useful guides of its kind. Its content intends to make the exercise of buying a new or used car in America today, as painless as possible.

Many unfamiliar and difficult situation can arise when buying and selling a new or used car. Though we have tried to cover the most important aspects of a car buying transaction, each situation is unique. Because of the many variables associated with an auto purchase or sale, always seek third party professional opinions for mechanical, financial, and legal matters. In most cases third party opinions will give you an accurate accounting of the facts. A third party opinion can also have a sobering affect on your decision, especially in situations where previous judgment may be influenced by emotions.

For most Americans, an automobile purchase is the second largest investment they will ever make, next to the purchase of a home. Therefore, proceed with extreme caution and careful contemplation. Never make a decision based on impulse.

This book is a handy guide, designed with easy access to serve the conscientious car buyer with accurate and clever tactics which can be used to strengthen your position when negotiating the final outcome of your next automobile purchase. You will discover on the pages heretofore, The Inside Secrets of Auto Dealers is the book to save you time and money, in this challenging environment known as the Automotive Industry.

CONTENTS

CONTENTS

CONTENTS

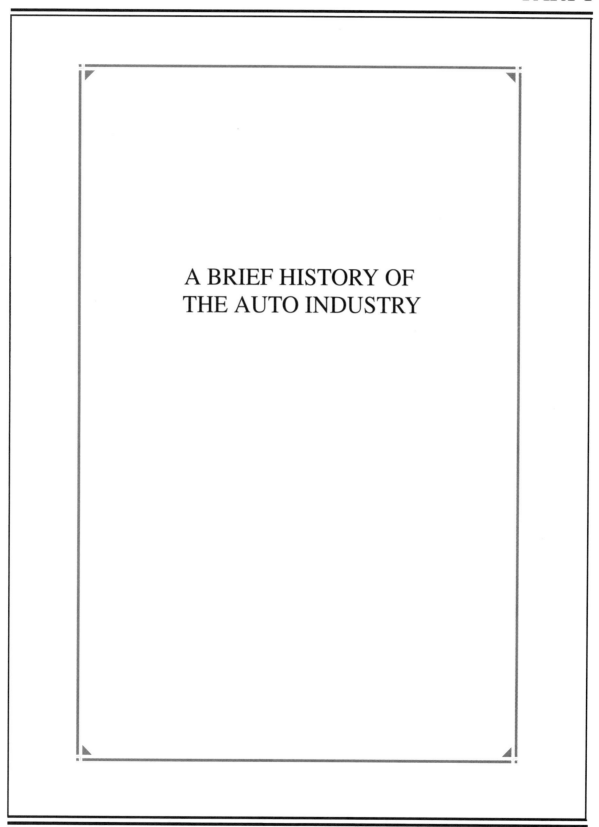

PART I

A BRIEF HISTORY OF THE AUTO INDUSTRY

Market History

New and used car sales, when looked at in combination, in any given United States market, show a surprising stability not often seen by standard economic indicators. These surveys take only new car sales into account when doling out the daily doom and gloom of the current economy. Yet, as all professionals within the industry will tell you, whenever new car sales are on the decline, a rise in used car sales is a predictable trend. Successful dealers direct their focus accordingly, thus keep pace with the market.

Because the automobile is still the number one means of transportation today, vehicles have become as big of a necessity to modern man or woman as soap or clothing, crossing all lines of age, gender, creed, and religion. Although small segments of the market can be keyholed to specific areas, as a whole, marketing prospectors consider the auto industry wide open territory. Hence, over 600 name plates (models) are offered in today's new car market, which is a trebled increase from a few years ago. The fierce competition among the manufacturers to meet consumer demand for constant change in style and quality, has had a dramatic affect on the price of new and used automobiles nationwide.

The fact that rising prices have outpaced normal inflation can be easily recognized by comparing the median-priced home and car of ten years ago to the median-priced home and car of today. This pricing frenzy seems to have unlimited boundaries. It is easy to envision the manufacturers continuing this trend well into the next millennium, making the price of a new car unimaginable. The used car market will follow suit, to the point where the Kelley Blue Book will be published in multiple volumes of books just to cover the numerous makes and models.

As the manufacturers continue to create an ever increasing need for reliable consumer assistance and information, another portion of the industry is doing everything in its power to halt the rising level of consumer education by using highly polished and complicated negotiating techniques. They utilize emotional manipulation and practices that, in any other business, would be considered highly unethical, if not criminal.

Because of the negative impact these old traditional practices and techniques have caused, many of today's educated and conscientious consumers have turned to alternative car buying methods, such as brokers, consultants, fleet and club buying services. Which do not always add up to be more advantageous than the traditional methods.

These services undoubtedly created with good intentions, have unfortunately fallen short of the mark for a variety of reasons. The auto brokers being the worse offenders of them all, due to the fact they prey on the consumers misconception that they can obtain vehicles below dealers cost (a falsehood, one the manufacturers will not allow). The reality is, they simply make arrangements with the auto dealers to buy vehicles at a reduced price, which in turn, they mark up and resell to the consumer. In addition to this atrocity, they make money off other profit centers as well, such as financing, exactly like the dealer. As a result of this method of doing business, they have become little more than off-site salespeople owing their allegiance to the dealership, not the consumer.

"Insider-type" programs as they are referred to in the business is a another problem area for the consumer. These programs offered by participating dealerships are nothing more than a pre-arranged agreement with large organizations or companies who offer their members discount car buying opportunities. Usually they are offered by insurance companies, membership shopping clubs, credit unions, professional associations, etc. Unfortunately they can be misleading even to the most savvy buyer.

Most consumers are familiar with the term "Fleet Price," which is an "Insider Type" program. This term among many is usually misunderstood by the average consumer who assumes the definition is "discount." Remember, these terms have been created by people inside the auto industry and do nothing more than give the dealership more opportunities to increase profits. In general, these types of programs lack specific information regarding trade-in values, finance rates, aftermarket options, and a variety of other items and extras that change with each buyer's particular situation.

These programs can be quite costly for the consumer if he or she is unaware of their content, mainly because they cause the consumer to lower their guard and subsequently be lulled into a false sense of security by associating familiar terms with discount or a special price. There are many dealerships who participate in these "Insider Type" programs. The problem is, there's no binding law or system of inspection in place that assures the consumer the dealer is actually following the terms and conditions of the agreement.

This allows the dealer to charge the consumer whatever he or she is willing to believe the so called special price really is. These "Insider Type" programs which the dealerships insist are in the interest of the consumer are actually self-serving. There is a later chapter in the book which explains each one of these topics in detail.

How It All Began:

The problems facing today's car buyers actually began some 50 years ago. The original architects who designed the selling process of automobiles looked to other industries to find the most successful negotiating tactics available. It didn't take long to find what is still revered today as the most effective method of negotiating; the third-party negotiator. A third-party negotiator is simply a fiduciary agent who works for you, or on your behalf, that is otherwise not involved in the situation. The greatest advantage to this type of arrangement is keeping emotional involvement separate from the issue at hand. A common practice in legal disputes, real estate transactions, politics and world economy.

After realizing the power of the third-party negotiator these industry pioneers decided to make a few small changes in an effort to increase the negotiating odds in their favor. Thus the infamous "Car

Salesman" was born. Next, they designed a compensation program that would give the salesperson the maximum incentive to negotiate at the lowest possible cost to their dealers. Hence, the "Sales Commission" was born.

To further insure their maximum interest the compensation program was based on a percentage of the profit rather than a percentage of the overall sales price. This stipulation in the compensation program would mark the beginning of the end of the fiduciary negotiator because the salesperson had an incentive to sell cars to the consumer at the highest possible price since his cut of the deal was based on the profit not gross. The following example is a typical ploy known by all car salespeople. However, because they are practitioners, it can sound quite believable to the unaware consumer who may not be able to identify this common ploy, as a sales tactic.

What salespeople try to do is instill your trust in them, then under the breath whisper in your ear, "Look Mr. or Mrs. Doe, I'm on your side. I'm gonna see if I can get the Sales Manager to go along with this deal because you all seem like honest hard working people." That's not at all what he's trying to do because the lower he goes on the sales price of the car directly causes his commission to be smaller. He's only creating the illusion that he is on your side.

By implementing this carefully planned deception as the foundation of today's automobile sales industry, which at its core is emotional manipulation, remains the cornerstone of everyday sales tactics. In the "Buyer Beware" chapter of the book we examine sales tactics at length.

A Look At Today's Market:

Small sparks of hope are beginning to appear all across the country which imply the new age of auto buying is here, such as General Motors', Saturn Division's, New Car Set Pricing Policy. Which is being coattailed by some new car dealership who advertise "no-hassle" car pricing. On the surface they appear to be positive steps in the right direction. Yet, when analyzed, it becomes painfully obvious they are nothing more than new marketing techniques designed to attract the help-starved consumer. But in the end, the results are the same as before. The dealer wants to wins.

To compensate for the "no hassle" buying program, the dealer offers the consumer less than market value for their trade-in, going from a new car dealer to a used car stealer. A similar tactic used by dealerships, now abolished by legislation, guaranteed minimum trade-in amount regardless of the vehicle's condition (usually $2,000.00 to $3,000.00).

In this scenario, the dealers were simply placing the pea under a different shell. To compensate for the loss they were taking on your trade-in, they would add that same amount to the sales price of the new car being purchased.

In the end it actually costs the consumer more money because it increased the total amount of taxable dollars. Other options available to consumers today are the "Insider Type" programs which we touched on briefly in the history chapter. "Fleet Service," which implies volume discounts are offered by membership shopping club, credit unions, insurance companies, etc., to their customers as a fringe benefit. These organizations are actually paid by the dealerships an average of $2,000.00 per month to advertise this service to their customers. The membership club or company will offer its customer, using a printed mail piece, a list of participating dealerships willing to sell new cars for a price less than what a non-member would pay.

The administrators of these programs, who work for the memberships clubs or companies, sign exclusivity agreements with dealers who are willing to pay their company for sending them new customers. The administrators, in turn tout this "free" service to their members, sending them to the participating dealers with nothing more than a brochure and their faith in the good name of the organization to which they belong.

It's perfectly legal because the company or club is fulfilling its obligation, as per the agreement, to the car dealership. Here again, by means of a reputable company lending its name to programs such as these, the customer is drawn into a false sense of security which leaves them susceptible to being more easily deceived. As most professionals in the industry will admit, the prices the dealer gives to the companies and clubs, who pass them on to their memberships as buying opportunities, rarely match the actual selling price of the car. It is a "low ball" tactic to get potential customers into the dealership.

How It Effects You:

1993 marked the 100th year of the automobile in America. For almost as long, confusion and distrust have been a prevalent factor among the American public. A good example can be found in the August 8th, 1936 issue of Automotive News which explains a city clerk in Richmond, Virginia was quoted as "being confused" about the trade-in value of eight horses and mules towards the purchase of 16 new trucks for the city. So, by no means is this a new problem.

Just as the Richmond, Virginia clerk encountered confusion, you will find the tactics used today are not so different. To become a better negotiator, keep in mind, all car salespeople are always attempting to confuse you.

PART II

HOW TO WIN NEGOTIATIONS

How To Win Negotiations

The very best way to win this game is by refusing to play. It is important to remember, sitting across the desk from you are trained professional negotiators. The odds are not in your favor. As discussed earlier the salesperson's claim to be "on your side," is a lie. He's on his side. He gets paid a percentage of the profit, not the overall selling price. Do not allow the salespeople to trick you into believing they are playing the role of a fiduciary agent.

Your best defense is to prepare yourself before ever entering the showroom. We suggest you do this by deciding in advance, your car purchase will be at the very least a two visit affair. Your first visit should be a fact finding mission, keeping in mind, you can make it a pleasant experience with the right attitude. Take a dozen demo rides, ask lots of questions and collect printed brochures that tell you about the car of your interest. But do not allow the salesperson to lead you into feeling guilty just because you are shopping for a new car, while in his mind, you should be buying one.

The salesperson may try to make you feel you are wasting his or her time because you are not ready to buy a car right now! That's their job. By firmly embracing the two visit rule, you will find the salesperson is the one who will become frustrated, not you.

Once you have obtained the information you're seeking, quietly leave the dealership. You will find it much easier to make the right decision when you are removed from the overwhelming temptation of immediate ownership. It is important for you to remember this basic human desire is the very point every salesperson in the industry is trained to invoke. You will find by removing yourself from their environment allows you the freedom to make rational decisions which are favorable to you. As you try to leave, the salesperson may try a tactic known as "the urgency factor."

Here is how it works. The salesperson will try and make you believe, for one reason or another, by leaving the dealership you will miss out on something you will not be able to get later. This is how they try to get you to buy "NOW." Regardless of their reasoning, no matter how believable it may sound, it's a tactic. In all the years I spent in the car business, I know the most disarming statement you the buyer can say to the salesperson is " Well, if that's the case, then I guess it's just not meant to be." This statement is almost impossible to overcome for the salesperson. How can you argue against fate?

Remember, there are thousands of dealers with millions of vehicles to choose from. If you miss on one, there will definitely be another. More important than the vehicle, is the reputation of the dealership and the individual trying to sell you a car. You will find that reputations are almost always based on the truth. The easiest way to verify their reputation is to find an appropriate time to go out to the service department by yourself and observe their method of doing business. Are there customers standing around who look unhappy or frustrated? If so, ask one for their opinion of the service since buying their new car. Would they buy another from the same dealer? How are they treated now that they own the car?, and so on. Be sure to get more than one opinion. Keep in mind there is no such thing as the perfect dealership. Just use fair and reasonable judgment.

Once you are comfortable with the dealership, begin looking for the best salesperson. This is not always the guy who sells the most cars. The best salesman is normally the one who has been at the dealership the longest. Normally, this person has a lot of experience in the car business and realizes the value of repeat customers and referral business. Sometimes he can be found working in the Fleet Department. The easiest way to find this person is by calling the dealership and asking the Sales Manager for the name of his top salesperson. This person is generally patient and willing to answer all of your questions. He or she will take an interest in you and your needs rather than an attitude that makes you wonder if their true destiny in life is herding cattle. And if this person is a good listener he or she will make logical recommendations based on the information you have given during the conversation.

Also remember, if you are buying a new or used car from a new car dealership ask to see their C.S.I. rating (customer satisfaction index). Because of the many problems dealerships have imposed on the industry, the factory developed the C.S.I. rating system as a service to the consumer. The C.S.I. rating system rates the performance of the dealership and the sales personnel based on each individual transaction. Rest assured if the dealer's representative makes excuses or is reluctant to show you their performance rating, it's probably because the rating is less than satisfactory.

PART III

BUYER BEWARE

Dealer Trade:

A dealer trade is exactly what it sounds like. It occurs when one new car dealer trades a car from their inventory with another new car dealer. It is a common practice encouraged by the factory and is done when a customer is looking for a new car in a certain color or option package and will not settle for anything less. Yet this is not always the best option for the buyer because he or she has no control over the transaction being conducted between the trading dealerships. First of all, the buyer doesn't know anything about the reciprocating dealer.

Although, federal law requires the dealerships to disclose any odometer discrepancy or collision repair, it does not always happen. Dealer trading has become a game played by Sales Managers. This is where one dealership's Sales Manager tries to pass one of their problem vehicles on to another. Unfortunately the loser of the game ends up being the buyer.

Another reason to avoid purchasing a dealer traded vehicle is the dealer loses what is known as "the factory hold back," which is a percentage of money (on an average--2%) the factory holds until the end of the year. This mean you will not get the same deal on the dealer traded car as you would if purchasing a car from the dealers in-stock inventory. To check and see if the vehicle you are interested in purchasing was traded from another dealer, simply look at the window sticker. It will state the name of the dealer who originally ordered the vehicle. It is not uncommon for some "swapped vehicles" to visit many dealerships before finding an unsuspecting recipient.

Factory Orders:

This is by far the best way to get exactly what you want on your new vehicle if you are able to wait . But you will find that most dealers prefer you buy one "now" and will try to entice you by telling you that you will get a better deal on one in stock. This is a common practice used by all new car dealers because they are paying interest on their cars in stock. They would much rather sell a car today at less profit than make a modest profit down the road on one which is ordered. It is true you may spend a few extra dollars by ordering a new car as opposed to settling for one being offered right then. Stop and consider the advantages. If you are like 90% of the buyers of a new vehicles, you'll be financing that new vehicle. A $200 savings today, will not be nearly as important two years later, nor will it effect your monthly payment considerably. If you stand firm and hang in there long enough most dealers will order you a new car for about $500.00 above cost. This is the way to go if time is not a factor. The dealer will tell you factory orders take about 6-8 weeks.The truth is closer to 12-14 weeks.

The waiting time varies depending on such things as the time of the year, (most automobile factories are closed for two weeks during Christmas and New Years) and how special the order.

The Payment Game:

The number one sales tactic used by new car dealerships focuses on diverting the buyer's attention from the actual sales price of the car to the monthly payment and down payment. BEWARE, do not play this game. To eliminate this trick is simple, just remember monthly payments are based on simple mathematical formulas. The information used in the formula is the selling price, plus tax, license and document fees.

Once you have obtained this information go to a third-party financial institution such as your bank for a second opinion. The bank can easily calculate your monthly payment, based on the cash down payment, current interest rates and the term length of the financing. A clearer understanding of this portion of the transaction can strengthen your position, when negotiating with the dealer.

Remember, they are professionals at this game and it is an area where the dealers excel in confusing most customers. Do not follow the salesperson down this road. You are the customer, you are in command of the negotiation and it's your money. The third-party opinion will allow you to detect any mathematical deception being posed by the dealer.

Aftermarket Accessories:

Due to the fact that consumers today are more concerned with the selling price of the car has enabled many car dealers more opportunities to establish additional profit centers, such as aftermarket accessories. It is not uncommon for a dealer to sell the new car buyer fancy body parts such as, plastic molding, door stripping and products that are supposed to make the paint last longer, which are all part of a so-called "protection package." Sometimes these aftermarket packages can cost as much as a thousand dollars extra.

Compounding these profit centers are stereos, alarms, and other electronic wizardry. Do yourself a favor, don't buy anything that was not put on the car at the factory. This will save you a serious amount of money. More important, aftermarket accessories are not always covered by the factory warranty which covers the rest of the vehicle. In some cases, aftermarket packages have actually been known to void the factory warranty. Your risk of loss by far outweighs your chance of satisfaction when considering after market accessories. Consider the following advice: buy your car from a car dealer and buy any aftermarket accessories from those who specialize in the sales of such items. There is no greater satisfaction than the feeling one gets when they have won at the car buying game. Do not spoil it with aftermarket accessory purchases.

Stealing Your Trade:

"Stealing your trade" is actual terminology used by professional car salespeople who get you to accept any amount less than the appraised value of your car. Remember they get paid on the profit of the sale of the new car plus a commission for convincing the buyer to accept less than the appraised value of their trade-in.

Your best bet, if you decide to trade your vehicle, is to look up the value of your car in any current Kelley Blue Book or N.A.D.A. Guide. The public library inventories the latest edition of each of these books in the reference department. Located in the front section of these books are explicit details which will guide you through the process of appraising your car. A visit with your friendly banker can also serve as an excellent source of access to this information.

Once you establish the value of your car, don't expect more. If you do, the dealer will have no choice but to raise the selling price of the car you are looking to buy. But once again, don't take any less.

Low Balling:

This dirty little ploy used by most new car salespeople is also known as "being put out on a bubble" or "let out on a screamer." But regardless what they call it, the end results will be the same; wasted time and aggravation. What the salesperson will do intentionally, is lie to you sometime before leaving the dealership by suggesting a sales price actually lower than the dealers cost. The tactic plants a number in your mind to remember. You can shop till you drop and no one will be able to come close to this price, because it was planted under the guise of a "low ball" tactic.

The intention is to lure you back to their dealership when you realize, after shopping the market for comparable prices, their price is unbeatable. Their hope lies in their own ability to convince you that an innocent mistake was made on their part. If you accept their rhetoric and decide to do business with them, the best you'll do is $50.00-100.00 less than the lowest bid of another dealer. If by chance you become a victim of this ploy, I firmly suggest, you leave that dealership and never return to its doorsteps again.

Year End Deals:

The established belief that one can save hoards of money by purchasing a new car under the guise of a so-called "year end deal," is a myth. Although it's not a bad way to get a good deal, the savings are negligible. The reason is an obvious one. New car dealers rarely lose money on the sale of a new vehicle. Also, consumers have a tendency to be less cautious of the dealership's year end offers because they believe the dealer is desperate to get rid of these car to make room for next year's new models.

The vehicles the dealer receives from the factory are only those he wants and has actually ordered for his inventory. The dealer does not have any car in his inventory that he does not want. Some of the largest profits ever made from a new car sale come from this type promotion. Also, consider that once the new year model is released, you have a year old vehicle. Buying into this belief, in effect, leads to paying a new car price for a used car. Keep in mind that new cars take their largest depreciation in the first year.

Leasing:

If you are completely unfamiliar with the concept of leasing, do not consider this program as an option. It will inevitably become a very expensive crash course with no return. After shopping a few different dealerships, it will become apparent they like leasing programs and will be suggested everywhere you go. There is a good reason for this. They make huge profits on lease deals. The main reason is they do not have to disclose the price of the car. They don't even call it a sales price. It's now known as a capitalization cost. Leasing does have some advantages but in general the word "savings" is not part of the formula.

If you wish to pursue a greater understanding of a lease program, start by asking the following questions:" What is the capitalization cost?", "What is the interest rate or lease factor ?", "Is it an open or closed end lease?", "What is the mileage limitation?"," How much will the mileage adjustment cost me at the end of the lease?", " If I have a trade-in, how does it fit into the deal?", " Can I have a full disclosure?". The best advise we can give you when considering a lease, is to do lots of homework, because each situation is unique.

The attraction of a lease begins when the salesperson employs the "payment game" tactic. Sure, monthly payment can be lower in a lease program, however at the end of the lease there is still a balance owed on the car. If you wish to buy this car at the end of the lease, you must refinance the residual balance, and the payment game begins again.

Fleet Department:

The fleet department is generally the best place to find the "easiest salespeople to work." People who work in the fleet department are commonly considered by the dealer as his "give away" personnel. The best way to find one of these salespeople is by calling the dealership and asking the Fleet Manager to recommend a salesperson in his department. Be sure you talk to the Fleet Manager because a regular salesperson could mislead you by saying "all of the salespeople are in the fleet department."

A customer does not have to be interested in purchasing an entire fleet of automobiles in order to buy a car from someone working in the fleet department. To qualify a dealership's claim to have a fleet department is simple. Ask the following questions: "Can you show me the dealer's invoice?", "Are you the person who approves the final agreed price?" Once at the dealership be sure his business card clearly states his title is "Fleet Manager." As a rule, fleet managers are usually senior salespeople. However, because this person is working in the fleet department is not a prerequisite for being a saint. They too are paid from the profit of the sale not the gross.

Keep in mind, most credit unions have fleet agreements with new car dealerships. So if you are a member of a credit union, it may be the best place to start. But once again, use caution. Once you establish your credit union has an agreement with a dealership of interest, go there and ask for a copy of the dealer invoice and have the Sales Manager write the agreed selling price on the invoice. Get it signed and take it to your credit union representative for validation.

Factory Invoice:

Yes, "factory invoices" really do exist. Will you ever see one? Probably not in this lifetime. During the ten years I spent in the auto business, I can honestly say, I have never seen a dealer make available the original invoices to even his own personnel. Sure, they will show you a photo copy of the original invoice, but I can tell you right now, as hard as it may be to believe, they make changes to them.

To verify if the photo copy of the dealer invoice is accurate takes very little effort. Adhered to the window of every new car is a factory sticker which lists all kinds of information about the car, such as the model number, optional equipment and dealer codes. As part of your research, the following list of instruction will help you determine the actual price as per the factory invoice. Go to the dealership after hours, which is not uncommon and perfectly legal. In fact, it's one of the reasons the dealership leaves the exterior light on all night.

At the top of the factory window sticker you will see several numbers. Write down the model number. It may say serial number -- every manufacturer uses a little different system -- but it's easy to find. Below that section look for the heading: "Optional Equipment." Listed below the heading are columns of words and numbers which describe the contents of the equipment package for that particular vehicle. Each line in the column will have a code number, the item (such as - anti-lock brakes), and the dollar amount for that particular item. Write down the code number of each item listed under the optional equipment section.

Go to a public library or bookstore and find an automobile consumer product book. Inside you will find the definition for each one of the codes, beginning with the model or serial number. To save yourself from aggravation, follow the step by step instructions in the book. It will show you how to add the items not listed on the sticker such as freight and dealer prep. It is not uncommon for the customer to misuse these books and arrive at a price that is thousands less than the actual dealer cost.

Dealer Added Sticker:

Dealer added stickers also know as "Addendum Stickers" appear on the window next to the factory sticker. Which by the way are intentionally designed to look like the factory sticker to deceive the consumer. Disregard these stickers all together, it's just another prop to make it easier to add more profit. The salespeople have all kinds of justifications, i.e. smoke and mirrors, for the additional sticker. They will tell you it is necessary to cover the high cost of running a large dealership, inflation, etc. Seeing the home of anyone who owns a new car dealership, will immediately tell you why the added dealer sticker appears on the window.

The Switch:

This little maneuver is an industry standard, but one that can be easily avoided by deciding on the type of vehicle you want before any discussion occurs that consider acting upon the sale. I can assure you, any car the salesperson tries to show you is for his gain, not yours. This tactic is normally executed after the salesperson has tried to make you believe the vehicle you are looking at is just to much money for your desired payment.

The switch is done by showing you an older flashy model that has more luxury items than the one shown first. My suggestion is take a look at it, test drive it, but do not buy it. Remember it's not the car you originally intended to buy, however it might be something to consider, if in fact price is a priority in your final decision. When it's time to consider all of the options, be sure you do it away from the dealership. It is just too easy to get caught up in the excitement of the moment and make a hasty decision you may regret the next day.

The Bump:

This is done in so many ways the only advice I can give you is "practice saying NO." Bumping a customer is simply getting the customer to believe the figure being discussed is an "out the door" figure. Once the customer agrees to the figure and a little time passes, the salesperson then asks, "how do you want to handle tax and license." Another way to bump the customer is by getting you to agree to a slightly higher payment or longer term finance contract.

In either case, it means the same thing, you pay more money. Every person working at the dealership plays the bumping game. It begins with the salesperson, if he can't bump you, the Assistant Sales Manager tries. If he fails, the Sales Manager takes a shot and if all the previous fail, you get to meet the General Manager. And to no surprise, he tries to bump you too.

Generally, this is where even the most experienced car buyer assumes the games is over. But it's not, the same process will occur when the customer meets the Finance Manager, and so on, and so on until you leave the dealership. The philosophy behind this tactic is as follows: as the customer is moved up the ladder of prestigious titles, they become intimidated. Don't let this happen. The General Manager of today may be a lot boy somewhere else tomorrow. Decide what you are willing to pay, offer that amount as the "out the door" price, no exception. If the powers at be agree, do the deal, otherwise leave. I guarantee you, by the time you get home, there will be a message on your recorder from the salesperson that suggests the negotiation is still open.

The Closer:

The closer, by far is the slipperiest creature you will ever meet. They are easy to spot. A firm hand shake, a warm smile, an easy going manner, a confident air, and a keen sense of humor, designed to immediately put you at ease, are the apparent traits. They appear to have the boy next door look and mannerisms. Yes, these guys have it all except one valuable ingredient, a conscience. These guys are good at what they do and are characterized by the dealers to be worth their weight in gold. Which is just about how much money they make each month.

Do yourself a favor, trust your instincts. If what this person says sounds to good to be true, it probably is. The best way to handle this person is to impose humility through a disarming statement. Tell this person you know he is the closer, therefore, "there's no need to jockey for position."

T.O.:

T.O. is short for "turn" or "turn over." All salespeople are trained professionals who carry an arsenal of tactical weapons which they use to keep you at the dealership as long as possible. T.O. is a tactic where the first salesperson begins introducing you to other salespeople, right down the line, until one says the golden word that turns you into a full blown sucker.

To stop this madness simply state to the initial salesperson that you understand how "T.O." works and would prefer to deal with only one individual. Should he attempt to continue playing this game let him know you will leave and find a dealer who does business your way.

Finance Manager:

The Finance Manager is undoubtedly the very best salesperson. He is easy enough to spot by the fact that he talks like a banker and tries to act like one. He is there for only one reason, to take as much of your money as he possibly can. He too gets paid commission on the profit of the sale, not the gross. His little office is where most people get taken the most.

The main selling tactic he imposes on you is fear. He will start by asking you a series of question, then he turns those question into possible scenarios that are motivated by fear of things that haven't even happened. It's a "what if" tactic. The purpose is to sell you protection against things that might happen in the future. Here are some examples: extended warranty, life, accident, and health insurance and protection packages.

The best way to disarm this person is to just say "no" to everything. Common sense will tell you what you must have to legally buy and own the car. i.e. title, bill of sale, insurance.

The Credit Game:

Once you have decided which vehicle you want to buy, the next step is filling out the credit application. If your credit is less than perfect the dealer will use this against you. This is done in an effort to make you believe you may not qualify the for the car you wish to purchase. Secondly, it gives the dealer a reason to suggest a larger down payment may be required or the interest rate may be higher.

In short, it makes it easier for the dealer to justify why they need more money without any responsibility for the action. It becomes very easy for the dealer to say: "it's not my fault you have blemishes on your credit report."

Do yourself a favor and seek financing BEFORE going shopping for a new car. As a pre-approved buyer, the dealer considers you a cash buyer which can lead to a better and cleaner deal. Also, it allows you the opportunity to focus on the deal itself.

IF I Could, Would You??:

The biggest advantage most car salespeople have over the consumer is the power of manipulation. Through a series of questions and answers the salesperson is manipulating you into a commitment, while at the same time, he remains uncommitted to you. Here's how the trap works: The salesperson will ask you, "If I could get you X amount of dollars for your car, would you buy today?" or "If I could get you the price you want, would you do business now?" The best defense against this tactic is to say, "why don't you see what you can do."

The reply is to reverse the tactic to your advantage. If you study the question and the reply closely, you will see the reply really didn't answer the question which keeps you uncommitted and at the same time he has obligated himself to come back with an answer. The commitment game is omnipotent among salespeople. Another verbal tactic might go something like this: "Your commitment to buy today arms me with the power to start the negotiation on your behalf." Remember, the negotiation is on his behalf.

No Hassle Pricing:

No hassle pricing is one of the newest tactics among the long line of marketing gimmicks used by new car dealerships. You will find "no hassle pricing" works to the dealers advantage, not yours. You are much better off going to a dealer who is not trying to dupe you in this fashion. Regardless of the dealer, you should resolve yourself to a " no hassle deal" by making one offer. If they take it, fine. If they do not, leave.

Where's The Profit?:

If you are like most normal Americans, you do not trust car salespersons or the dealers for one reason or another. Usually it's because they are simply not trustworthy. Like any game that's been played for more than fifty years, it evolves. During this evolutionary process the leaders in the industry figured out that it was more advantageous to spread the profit throughout the various stages of buying an automobile rather than lumping it into just the selling price of the car. So understand, once the selling price of the vehicle has been established, focus on trade-in allowance, financing, warranty cost and dealer accessory packages.

First Time Buyer Programs:

If you are a first time buyer, there are special programs designed just for you. They are designed to help individuals who have not had the opportunity to establish a credit history to purchase a new car. Unfortunately, you will find most dealers are less than enthusiastic about these programs, mainly because they are limited to a specific profit margin. Who can qualify for one of these programs? Generally, people who are under the age of twenty-five. What are the basic requirements to qualify for one of these programs? The basic requirement is to have at least one year of continuous employment, no derogatory credit, and 20 to 30 percent down.

They also have top limits on spending regardless of your income. Generally, first time buyer programs are limited to entry level vehicles. These are factory designed programs which help them establish long term name plate loyalty. These programs, as a rule, also carry stiffer insurance coverage requirements.

Under The Ether:

I am quite sure this cliche has some measure of truth to it basically because of the power of the human emotion. Putting you under the ether is what every salesperson is expected to do to you from the moment you walk in the front door of the dealership. And it is a constant under-tow during the presentation, demonstration, and eventually the negotiation. By design, it starts with the shiny new paint and the new car smell and finishes with getting every dollar of your money they possibly can.

The technique is like a machine designed to anesthetize you. Does it work? You bet it does. History has proven the longer the salesperson can keep you at the dealership, betters the chance that you will buy a new car. And do it at a price which is more desirable for them.

Believe it or not, some dealers have been known to keep customers waiting 5 to 6 hours. And then have them spend another 2 hours with the Finance Manager for a final wringing out of the wallet. The best advice I can give, is to let the salesperson know that your time is valuable and important to you. Usually, an hour is more than enough time to complete the entire transaction.

PREPARING YOURSELF

Preparing yourself:

Preparing yourself is a must when dealing with an auto dealer. It is important to remember, that salespeople practice their routines everyday. Which makes them far more proficient at the game of manipulation than the one time or even annual car buyer. Part of their game plan relies on your lack of knowledge and expertise in this area. What you have in your favor is: selling automobiles is not done by rocket scientists. Use it to your advantage.

As a rule, most of the applicants for sales positions, which I have interviewed, have average intelligence or less. Recruiting extremely smart people to join the ranks of the sales staff, was near impossible. By preparing yourself and doing your homework, you will find most salespeople do not possess an unusual power of persuasion. In fact, they flounder when dealing with a customer who knows what they want. To help you prepare yourself with a winning attitude, the following instructions will guide you through the decision making process and equip you with the appropriate tactics to disarm even the slipperiest salesperson.

Deciding What You Want:

Half the battle is knowing what type of vehicle you want to buy before you actually go to the dealership. You can do this by observing cars on the road, in shopping mall parking lots and other public places. Buy a new car magazine that features the car of your choice to learn more about it. Today, the process has become more complicated than ever before because there are more choices. By asking yourself the following questions, you can eliminate a great number of vehicles, rather quickly. You will find, by answering the following questions before you shop, will make it easier to find the car that is right for you.

1. Am I interested in a new or used vehicle?
2. What type of vehicle best fits my transportation needs? (Car-Truck-Van-Mini van- etc.)
3. Am I interested in a specific make and model?
4. What type of equipment is a must? (Automatic-A/C-Tilt wheel- etc.)
5. What other optional equipment would I like? (Power windows-Cruise-AM/FM radio- etc.)
6. What will be my primary use of this vehicle? (commuter-Work-Pleasure)
7. Is gas mileage a concern?
8. Will anyone else in my family be using this vehicle? (What are their needs)
9. What color do I want?

What You Need To Bring:

As I have stated before, you are in a much better position at the dealership if you secure your own financing prior to the visit. Should you elect to choose the dealer to secure your financing, you can save yourself hours of needless aggravation by coming prepared. Below is a list of item most dealers must acquire from the customer to complete a sales transactions. In certain cases, the dealership may require documentation other than what's listed below.

1. Current registration and title for your car - if trading.
2. Loan account number and current pay-off amount on your trade. (call your current lien holder)
3. Current paycheck stubs or your most recent tax return.
4. Account numbers and balances on all current monthly financial obligations.
5. A written explanation of any past credit problems.
6. The names, addresses and phone numbers of at least 3 personal references.
7. Your current drivers license and social security card.
8. Proof of current automobile insurance.

A Pad Of Paper And A Pen:

It may sound like I am being a bit cynical, but carrying a note pad and pen is a good idea and if nothing else, an excellent prop. Believe me when I tell you nothing takes the wind out of an aggressive salesperson's sail as quickly as this little prop. This is what is known in the car business as the "clip board syndrome." The pad and pen are easily accessible tools known by salespeople nationwide as the beacon of customer intelligence.

This small little secret carries an extremely profound psychological effect on the salesperson because he or she identifies you as a "shopper" as opposed to a perspective mark. I cannot tell you how effective this really is. It also helps you keep track of all the different individuals you deal with and tracking the different vehicles at different dealerships. Even if you do not take a single note, carry it anyway, as a prop.

The most helpful information to jot down while shopping is:

1. The dealership's name and location.
2. The name of the salesperson
3. The dealer stock numbers on the vehicle as well as the last 6 digits of the I.D. number.
4. The years, makes, models, and colors.
5. The current odometer reading (mileage).
6. The number of cylinders.
7. Type of transmission (manual or automatic)
8. Equipment and additional features.

9. Retail asking price.
10. Any price variations you are quoted.

Finding The Right Dealer:

As stated earlier, it is a good idea for the consumer to shop for a good reputable dealer first. The best way to do this is call and ask to talk to the General Manager. You may be unsuccessful reaching this individual on the first try since it is their nature to divert query calls to someone else. However, with a little persistence you will get through. You should get to know this person for the reasons previously explained and if there is a problem with the car you ultimately purchase, thereafter. This is especially true should the problem require any financial expenditures by the dealerships. The General Manager is normally the only one authorized by the dealer to spend dealership money. Once you have made contact with the General Manager, the following list of questions will give you a good idea of the dealership's capabilities.

1. What new vehicle lines do they offer?
2. Do they have full service capabilities?
3. Do they have their own parts department?
4. Do they have their own bodyshop or do they sublet the work?
5 What are their hours for: Sales, Parts, and Service?
6. Do they offer weekend service?
7. What warranty if any do they offer on their used vehicles?
8. What is the standard factory warranty on the new vehicles they offer?
9. Do they have a fleet department?
10. Do they offer financing if so, will it address any special needs you may have?
11. Does their dealership offer any unique features not found elsewhere?
12. If you were unhappy after your purchase, would you be free to contact him again directly?

Getting Your Fair Trade-in Value:

Trade-in value is one of the most feared topics of the average consumer. The reason being, for years dealers have led consumers into believing the trade-in is just another piece of the overall transaction. When in fact, they are two separate transactions. First, the sale of the new vehicle and second, the purchase of your vehicle. The consumer will be less susceptible to being gouged if he or she can maintain the separation of the transactions. You would not believe how many trusting souls take the word of the dealer when establishing trade-in value. I have seen literally hundreds of deals where the customer did their homework and got a new car at a fair price, then turn around and accept thousands less than the fair market value of their vehicle. Trust me when I tell you that, if allowed, the dealers will give you less than fair market value for your vehicle. As we discussed earlier, go to a public library or ask your bank the current value of your car as rated in the Kelley Blue Book or N.A.D.A. Guide.

Before Buying A New Car:

One thing you must always remember, car salespersons will tell you what you want to hear, every-time. Everyone from the General Sales Manager to the rookie salesperson make their living telling people what they want to hear. I have trained hundreds of salespeople and I can assure you the common interest among them is learning psychological tactics, not product knowledge. Salespeople have to be forced to learn product knowledge word by word.

Automobile history tells us there is a certain romance between man or woman and machine. And because of this fact, naturally we want to know as much as possible about our upcoming new love. A manufacturer's brochure is a good place to start learning about the car you wish to buy. The brochure contains every aspect of the car, the facts and the romance. It contains performance specification, safety features and luxury items. Use independent sources as well to learn more about the car such as, automotive periodicals.

Product knowledge can be a useful advantage over the salesperson. It can help you determine his experience level and integrity. By gaining this advantage will narrow your focus considerably. And finally never lose sight of your goal, which is "TO WIN" at the game.

The Ad Game:

Open any weekend newspaper and you will find an advertisement for just about every brand of automobile sold in America today. Most of the ads contain some kind of hook, designed to lure you onto the showroom floor of the dealership. Unlike other merchandise ads who are offering a truth in advertising campaign, the automobile dealer's ads are selling the same thing their salespeople sell: rhetoric!

This wildcatter's approach to advertising has imposed legislation to protect the consumer. But, as with all laws someone figures out a new way to skin a cat. This has been especially true in television advertising. Have you ever tried to read a manufacturer's disclaimer when it appears on the television screen during a commercial? You will be amazed by what you find.

The best way to utilize competitive advertising is to take the advertisement of one dealer to another. Get a written quote that states their price then go to another dealer for a competitive quote using the previous quote as the one to beat. It called beating them at their own game.

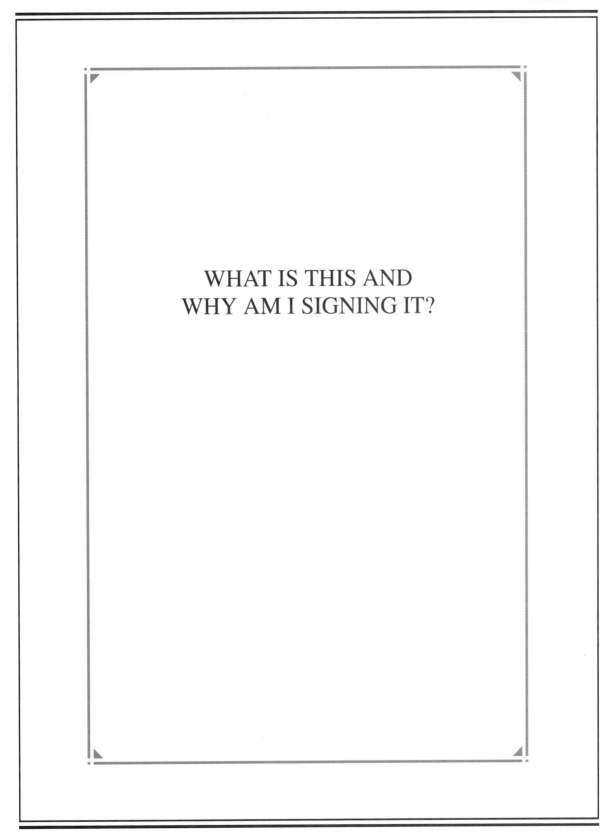

PART V

WHAT IS THIS AND
WHY AM I SIGNING IT?

What Is This? And Why Am I Signing

Most forms used by licensed dealers are printed by Law Printing. They are standardized forms that conform to the law and are written to protect the buyer against fraud and deception. To verify the dealership is using a document printed by Law Printing, simply look to the lower left hand corner. There will be a "Law Printing" logo followed by the form number and state to which it applies.

The most important document you will be asked to sign is the Purchase Order or Security Agreement. This is the form that outlines the particulars of the deal. Fortunately, there are laws that stipulate the limits of the agreement which are binding and cannot be changed or manipulated by either party.

In order to assist you through this endless maze of paperwork, we have included a numerical outline which explains each item of a Standard Purchase Order or Security Agreement. And though some contracts may be slightly differently, we have tried to cover the areas that can make the greatest difference in the final outcome of the contract. Because these are legal documents, do not sign anything you do not fully understand. It is always a good idea to make sure the document you are about to sign is complete and you fully understand its content. The most scrupulous car buyer will have the representative's of the dealer who sign the contract also print their names.

The Purchase Order/Security Agreement:

This is the long "contract" looking document. Starting at the top you will see a place for:
(1) Stock Number:
(2) Source:
(3) Salesman:
These items are for the Dealer's internal information.

Next you will see:
(4) Seller's name and address:
(5) Buyer's name:
(6) Buyer's residence and business address:
(7) Residence and Business phone numbers:

It is a good idea to carefully review the contract to be sure the information you have provided is correct. These forms are computerized which causes the information to transfer to other documents as it is written. So whatever is written on the first document, will appear on every document thereafter, including the registration.

Next you will see the following words:

(8) DISCLOSURES PURSUANT TO THE "TRUTH-IN-LENDING ACT"

The five sections in the box directly below this heading must be filled in prior to signing the contract. Pay close attention to this section because these five boxes contain the most pertinent information about the deal.

(9) THE FIRST SECTION - "ANNUAL PERCENTAGE RATE"

This is your actual yearly interest rate. If you are not happy with this rate and think you can do better at your own bank, ask the Finance Manager for an "option" (usually 10 days) to shop the rate.

10) THE SECOND SECTION - "FINANCE CHARGE"

This is the total interest you will pay, excluding late fees or revisions, if the contract goes full term. Since interest is usually figured either by the rule of 78 or according to the sum of periodic time balances, if paid early you will be entitled to an interest refund. In short, you are only charged interest for the amount of time you use the money, the sooner you pay it off, the less interest you pay.

(11) THE THIRD SECTION - "AMOUNT FINANCED"

This is the amount you are asking the financial institution to loan. By keeping a careful eye on this section you can keep the Finance Manager from "Bumping" you.

(12) THE THIRD SECTION - "TOTAL OF PAYMENTS"

This is simply taking the payment you agreed to pay and multiplying it by the term. (i.e. $200.00 per month x 60 months = $12,000)

(13) THE FIFTH SECTION - "TOTAL SALE PRICE"

This is the total cost of the car including down payment, interest, tax, license and accessories. Unfortunately, a large portion of this number is usually interest. Unless you can afford to pay cash, finance charges are a necessary evil.

Next you will see:

(14) "YOUR PAYMENT"

This states you agree to:
(15) Number of payments
(16) Amount of payments
(17) When the payments are due

(18) NOTE: If you ask for or were offered "an option" to check your own finance source, it must be noted in this section. It will read 60 payments at (agreed amount) or one payment of (amount financed) due seven or ten days from the contract date. This box also contains an explanation of:

(19) Security
(20) Late Charges
(21) Prepayment

(22) "NEW/USED"

This refers to the vehicle you are buying. Check it carefully to make sure it contains what you agreed to purchase.

(23) New/Used
(24) Year
(25) Make
(26) Number of Cylinders
(27) Diesel, gas or other

(28) Body style

(29) Model

(30) Odometer Reading

(31) Vehicle Identification Number

(32) Color

(33) Trim

(34) Tires

(35) Transmission

(36) Key Number

(37) License Number

(38) Report of Sale Number

(39) At this point you will notice 2 columns begin. Let's take the right column first. It will state:

(40) "AS IS" or "SOLD AS PER DUE BILL" it will describe a particular item, such as, Am/Fm Cassette, etc.

Below this is:

(41) ITEMIZATION OF "AMOUNT FINANCED"

SECTION 1

(42) (A) "CASH PRICE MOTOR VEHICLE AND ACCESSORIES"

This is the total dollar amount of the car and any additional items you have purchased, such as alarms, Am/Fm Cassette, paint guard, fabric shield, moldings, etc. Although most Finance Managers "Disclose" the accessories being purchased by line item, there is the occasional bad penny. Make sure this is the price you agreed to pay. Remember a payment that starts at $201.00 before the alarm and moldings is now $218.00. While $17.00 extra per month doesn't sound bad, over a 60 month contract, it actually adds up to $1,020.00....and that buys a lot of gas.

(43) CASH PRICE MOTOR VEHICLE AND ACCESSORIES

The Finance Manager should itemize the cost (i.e. $10,820 would be $10,020 for the vehicle and $800 in accessories.) Unfortunately, this is not always done. Keep in mind, you can not be forced to buy any accessories you do not want.

(44) (B) DOCUMENT "PREPARATION CHARGE" (up to maximum allowable by law)

This is a dealer fee which is usually non-negotiable....so save your strength for bigger battles.

(45) (C) SMOG FEE PAID TO SELLER.

This applies to a used vehicle when a "Used Report of Sale" is used. There could be many reasons to use a "Used Report of Sale" such as demo, factory car, or an "unwind." This fee is generally accepted as a non-negotiation item.

(46) (D) SALES TAX.

The sale tax is culminated by adding all lines above, then multiplied by the current tax rate.
For example:
10,000.00 - Car
    300.00 - Accessories
     35.00 - Documentation
     26.00 - Dealer Smog
10,361.00 - TOTAL
The total is then multiplied by the current state sales tax rate.

(47) (E) LUXURY TAX.

This is a federal tax charged on any amount over $30,000.00. It is figured at a rate of 10%, and is applicable only on any amount over $30,000.00, not the total amount. Luxury Tax Rate: 10%

(48) (F) SERVICE CONTRACT (optional).

This is the price of any extended warranty you have added to the purchase price of the car. There are many kinds of warranties on both new and used cars. Make sure you understand all of your options before settling on a warranty. This could spare you lots of trouble and expense in the future.

We strongly recommend you give serious consideration to the warranty being offered by the dealer. Even though your credit union, bank or insurance company may offer mechanical breakdown warranties, they do not administer or honor the aftermarket policies. The warranty being offered by the dealer is definitely honored by him and usually covers much more. Do yourself a favor, spend a little extra money for a good warranty. When compared to other industry warranties, the auto industry has one of the least expensive rates. (i.e. $695.00 [6%] on a $12,000 car -vs- $69.00 [17%] on a $399.00 television). Remember, it is not "if " your car will ever break, it is "when." In short, extended warranties are worth buying.

(49) (G) OTHER AND TO WHOM PAID.

This is a clause which is rarely used. Occasionally in the event of a high payoff on a lease turn-in, or a revolving credit card account, or bank loan, the financial institution may require the applicant to pay off the item in question in order to approve financing. Caution....any amount entered here, unless offset by a matching down payment will go into the amount financed and therefore increasing your monthly payment.

Next you will see:
(50) TOTAL CASH PRICE (A - G)

This is a subtotal of everything in Section 1.

SECTION 2

(51) "AMOUNTS PAID TO PUBLIC OFFICIALS"

This section applies to licensing fees which are non-negotiable and are set by your states D.M.V.

(52) (A) "LICENCE"

The license fee can range anywhere from a simple $9.00 transfer fee to hundreds of dollars depending on the current status of the records. The latter, refers to purchasing a used car. The Department of Motor Vehicles dictates this amount and does not allow a dealer to over charge for it. This number is an estimate to the best of the dealer's ability. The actual fee charged by the D.M.V. could be lower or higher than this estimate, so you will receive a check or a bill for the difference if it is not correct. D.M.V. fees are non-negotiable and are the buyer's responsibility to pay.

(53) (B) "REGISTRATION" - This is normally included in (A) "LICENSE."

(54) (C) "SMOG IMPACT FEE"

Currently this fee in California is $300.00 and is assessed on any used vehicle that was not originally built for California and has not been registered in California in the last 12 months (out of state vehicles). This fee is a one time charge. You will not have to pay it with each renewal. Let us point out however, that out of state vehicles bring with them their own set of special problems, such as, rust from road salt, salt water oxidation, missing smog equipment, and occasionally miles that have been turned back by the previous owner. When selecting an out of state vehicle, use extreme caution. Get a thorough diagnostic check as well as the history of the car before proceeding. Take your time. You can be sure the dealer did.

(55) "TOTAL OFFICIAL FEES" These are simply the total charges paid to the D.M.V.

SECTION 3

(56) "AMOUNT PAID TO INSURANCE COMPANIES"

The only comment on this section is simply when buying a car, see a dealer and when buying insurance, see an insurance agent. We do not recommend (other than the occasional 30 day binder which allows you to take delivery of the vehicle) buying Life, Accident and Health Insurance Policies while purchasing an automobile because they are usually overpriced for the coverage you receive. The premium can raise your monthly payment as much as $100.00. We recommend seeing your own agent and taking out a "Term Life Policy." Although term life policies will not cover you for accident and lost wages, you can buy a $100,000 policy for under $50.00 per month. Just plain good sense says "no" to this option.

(57) "SMOG CERTIFICATION FEE PAID TO STATE"

This is the fee the dealer must remit to the state of California for the actual "smog certificate." This amount varies from state to state. To find out your state's current charge call your local D.M.V.

(58) "TOTAL (1 - 4)"

This is the total cash price of the car. If you were to write one check with no trade-in for the automobile being purchased, this line would be the amount.

(59) SECTION 6 - This entire section deals with your down payment calculation.

(60) (A) Trade-in (and Description)

This section outlines the year, make, model, vehicle identification number, and mileage of your trade. Check it carefully. You do not want your 1986 year car appraised as a 1985 year car, or have money deducted from your trade-in over misread mileage.

(61) Further to the right, a line with the letter (A) is shown, which is where your trade allowance is recorded - regardless of what your payoff agreement is with the dealer. This is the amount the dealer is actually paying for your trade-in. This is an area where a lot of fast talking is done to divert you from this item. Make sure the amount shown is the same as promised. The normal razzle dazzle is they are reducing the price of the new car by the same amount as the trade.

(62) (B) "LESS PAY OFF"

What this means is if your trade is worth $5,000 and you still owe your bank $2,000.00, the dealer must pay off the balance in order to obtain a clear title.

Note: This is usually an estimate that you are responsible for (i.e. if the contract states a $2,000.00 pay off and it turns out to be $2,511.00, you will pay the difference to the dealer.) We recommend that you call the lein holder and get the pay off amount. Ask the lein holder for a 10 day pay off. A 10 day pay off will be the amount of the pay off 10 days from the day you call. This gives you time to complete your new car transaction.

(63) (C) "TRADE-IN (A less B)"

This is the "net" value of your car after the dealer subtracts your pay off amount from the amount being paid by the dealer. Occasionally the pay off is higher than the actual appraised value. This is known as negative equity and will be deducted from your cash down payment or added to the amount financed. Just because a dealer says the deal includes paying off your trade does not mean that's what it is worth. If a negative equity situation does arise, take your time and make sure you understand exactly what is going on or you may end up in worse shape on the car you're buying when it comes to trading the next time.

(64) (D) "DEFERRED DOWNPAYMENT DUE BEFORE 2ND INSTALLMENT PAYMENT"

In this space is where the dealer will show any remaining down payment you owe when the transaction is complete. This is known as a "pick-up payment" and because of trade situations, a partial down payment or derogative credit, the bank may require a higher than normal percent down. A lot of dealers understand this and will actually give you additional time to pay off down payments (usually not longer than 21 days).

I recommend you carefully assess your financial situation and make sure that you can live up to the committed "pick-up payments" simply because some folks, in the heat of the moment, have been known to bite off more than they can chew. However, if you are comfortable with the deferred down payment arrangement, then do it because it lowers your amount financed, which in turn lowers your monthly payment. Also, there is usually no interest charged on these "pick-up payments."

(64)(A) "MFR'S REBATE"

This is where you sign the manufacturer's rebate to the dealer and the dealer applies the same amount to your down payment. To make sure you're getting the deal you were sold, check the Cash Price

(#42), less the figure in this space.

This is the actual price of the car (i.e., cash price $11,500 plus fees less manufacturer's rebate $700. $11,500-$700=$10,800) Note: you are paying sales tax on the cash price before rebate. This is appropriate and the way most state sales tax laws specify it must be done.

(65) (F) "REMAINING CASH DOWNPAYMENT"

This is simply the money you are putting towards the down payment at the time of the transaction, whether it is cash, check or credit card. Remember, the more money you can afford to put down means smaller payment and savings on finance charges.

(66) (F) (6) "TOTAL DOWNPAYMENT (6C+D+E+F)"

This amount is calculated by taking your negative or positive equity from your trade plus your "deferred down payment (pick-up payment)" and adding to your cash down payment. Heretofollow are two examples, one showing positive equity, one showing negative equity in the trade.

POSITIVE EQUITY IN TRADE:

A. Trade-In (Description)
   Yr.88 Make Ford
   VIN 1FA8270HOL624796
   Model Taurus $ 6,750.00   (Allowance)
   Odometer 76,531
B. Less Pay-Off $ <2,750.00> (B)   (Brackets indicate negative numbers)
C. Trade-In (A less B) $ 4,000.00   (C)
D. Deferred Downpayment
   due before 2nd Install. $ 400.00   (D)
E._____ $ (E)
F. Remaining Cash Downpayment $ 1,500.00   (F)

TOTAL DOWN PAYMENT $ 5,900.00   (This would be the total down payment)

NEGATIVE EQUITY IN TRADE:

A. Trade-In (Description)
   Yr.<u>88</u> Make <u>Ford</u>
   VIN <u>1FA8270HOL624796</u>
   Model <u>Taurus</u> $ <u>6,750.00</u>   (Allowance)
   Odometer <u>76,531</u>
B. Less Pay-Off $ <u><7,750.00></u> (B)   (Brackets indicate negative numbers)
C. Trade-In (A less B) $<u><1,000.00></u>   (C)
D. Deferred Downpayment
   due before 2nd Install. $ <u>400.00</u>   (D)
E.<u>_____</u> $<u>_____</u>   (E)
F. Remaining Cash Downpayment $ <u>1,500.00</u>   (F)

<u>TOTAL DOWN PAYMENT</u> $ <u>900.00</u>   (This would be the total down payment)

Keep in mind the amount "owed" on an automobile does not mean it's worth that amount. With to-day's longer term financing, it is not uncommon to be "upside down" in your trade or owe more on the car than it is actually worth. If you are faced with this situation, carefully consider whether trading at this time is really to your advantage. In most cases it will only put you in worse shape on the car you are buying.

(67) "AMOUNT FINANCED (5 less 6)"

This is once again the amount you will be borrowing from the bank. Please note this figure should be the same as the amount noted in the "Truth-in-Lending Act" box. Take your time and review (41) , the "Itemization of Amount Financed," numbers 1 through 7. This is the most important information contained in the contract because it is the amount of money you are liable for. If you have any questions, make sure you ask the Finance Manager and be sure you are comfortable with the answers before continuing. In most cases, the amount is a considerable sum of money and a long term commit-ment on your part. Remember, it's your time and your money, therefore, there is no such thing as a stupid question.

(68) "PREPAYMENT REFUND"

This section explains the method of calculation the financial institution will use to figure any interest rebate owed in the event of an early payoff.

(69) "VEHICLE USE" Personal or Commercial

If you are buying a vehicle for commercial purposes carefully read the back of the contract. It may greatly restrict your usage of the vehicle.

(70) "SERVICE CONTRACT"

This section is where you will sign if you decide to purchase an extend warranty. Most service contracts sold on used cars must be purchased at the time of sale (an extremely smart option when buying a used automobile). Unlike used car purchases, you have up to one year to decide on additional coverage when purchasing a new car.

(71) "SELLER ASSISTED LOAN"

This is rarely used anymore. It's only relevant if the dealer secures a separate loan for your down payment. But today with 0 down financing (O.A.C.), this is not really necessary.

(72) "LEGAL OWNER"

This usually remains blank until the dealer has final bank approval. This is where your lending institution's name will appear. The dealer may put their name in this space if you are paying by check (until it clears the bank) or if you still owe money or trade documents to the dealer. Once you have fulfilled the obligation to the "legal owner" they must surrender the title over to you according to the agreement. Directly below the "Vehicle Description Box" you will see:

(73) "NOTICES"

This statement is to verify that the buyer listed on the top of the contract will receive all correspondence and notices regarding this transaction.

NOTE: On some contracts there maybe an explanation of what is referred to as a "buyers guide." This pertains to used vehicles and are supposed to be affixed to the window of any used vehicle for sale by the dealer. It should be placed on the vehicle prior to test driving the car. The Buyer's Guide sticker is extremely useful because it describes the warranty coverage offered by the dealer, as well as a list of problems the car may have.

(75) "STATEMENT OF INSURANCE"

NOTE: You do not have to buy auto insurance from the dealer as a prerequisite to obtain financing. You have the right to choose your own insurance agent or company to provide the necessary insurance coverage. Beware: if you do not provide insurance as agreed to in the contract or it lapses, the dealer or bank may automatically add insurance fees to the existing obligation and it is almost guaranteed to be more expensive than coverage obtained on your own..

This will be implemented only when purchasing automobile insurance from the dealer. If you are providing your own insurance, make sure it has the word "none" typed in the space, then initial it and have the dealer initial it as well.

(76) "CREDIT INSURANCE AUTHORIZATION AND APPLICATION"

Do yourself a favor and see an insurance agent before purchasing this type of policy. You will be much better off purchasing a separate term life policy which offers more coverage at a fraction of the cost. This is one of the many ways the consumers ends up paying large sums of money for items than can be purchased elsewhere at a fraction of the cost. By far the worst part of this scenario is the dealer is the one who profits the most not the insurance company. This type of insurance it not legally require.

(78) "OFFICIAL FEES"

This states that you will pay the D.M.V. transfer fee to obtain the title once the lien is satisfied.

(79) What appears next on most contracts is a recommended course of action a buyer can take should there be a complaint.

(80) Below this, most documents explain your rights. It states the seller or finance company cannot change this agreement without your written consent. But, also keep in mind if financed, the deal is subject to the credit lender's approval and occasionally the bank will require that the deal be restructured to meet its specification. A dealer may, if required by the bank, call you back in and ask you to sign a new, mutually agreed contract. But BEWARE this is also used as a ploy by some dealers to get you back in just so they can sweeten their deal.

(80)(A) "NOTICE OF RECISION RIGHTS" (If it's a security agreement you're signing)

Under Section K on the reverse of the contract it will state if the dealer cannot secure financing on your behalf and you must return the vehicle to the dealer, they are obligated by law to return your money and trade-in.

There is a general misconception regarding the rights of recision among the general public.Most people believe you have 3 days to make up your mind whether to keep the new car or return it. This is not true. Once you sign the documents and take physical delivery and the dealer fulfills his end of the bargain, it is a finished deal.

(81) Printed in red type is the minimum Public Liability Insurance Limits law and by signing in this space means you understand you are to provide liability insurance and neither the bank nor dealer are responsible for providing this coverage. You are obligated to meet the lender's minimum requirements on Comprehensive and Collision insurance for the full term of the finance agreement.

(82) Next is your statement that you have read and understand both sides of this agreement and have received a copy.

(83) This space is where you sign to verify that you will comply with the terms and conditions of the contract. Let us stress once again, DO NOT SIGN until you are completely satisfied and understand your obligation.

Additional Forms You May Be Asked To Sign:

"AGREEMENT TO FURNISH INSURANCE"

This form simply states that you understand and agree that while your vehicle is financed you must keep it fully insured at all times. If you do not, the lien holder has the right to add V.S.I. (Vendor's Single Interest) Insurance. This is their legal right and you can be sure they will execute it should your policy lapse.

"ODOMETER DISCLOSURE STATEMENT"

This form is your assurance from the dealer the mileage on the odometer represents the actual mileage on the car and he has not tampered with it.

NOTE: There are two boxes on this form and if either one is checked, the dealer is disclosing to you: (1) The speedometer has turned over, so if it reads 36,451 and this box is checked, that means the car has 136,451 or,

(2) The mileage on the car is not correct for whatever reason (speedometer changed, disconnected, etc.), so you have no way of knowing the true mileage. Use extreme caution whenever entering either of these situations.

"THE NINE PACK" (Form #951)

This applies to your trade. You will be asked to sign any of 7 different forms which relate to your trade-in situation.

1st - Your odometer statement to the dealer.
2nd - This is your bill of sale to the dealer that releases it from you to them.
3rd - This is your authorization to the dealer to pay off any existing lien so they can obtain a clear title.
4th & 5th - "Payoff Adjustment"
This states when negotiating the deal you and the dealer were using a set number for your bank payoff. If it turns out the payoff is actually higher, you agree to pay the difference. If it is lower the dealer will refund you the difference.
6th & 7th - "Power of Attorney"
These allow the dealer to sign any documents or paperwork on your behalf that pertain to the release of the title or registration of your car.

"DUE BILL" OR "WE OWE"

This is any item purchased as an accessory or aftermarket package which has to be installed on the car. (i.e., add stereo and alarm). If no aftermarket products or accessories are purchased, you will probably be ask sign this form verifying that fact.

"NOTICE TO CO-SIGNER"

If you are co-signing for someone, read this form thoroughly. It is self-explanatory. In short it states if for any reason the signer does not fulfill his or her obligation you, the co-signer are "fully responsible" for the debt no matter who has possession of the car.

"POWER OF ATTORNEY"

You will probably be asked to sign 2 copies. They are for the dealer's D.M.V. clerk so he/she can sign the appropriate paperwork to transfer the title of the vehicle you're buying into your name.

"R.O.S. (Report of Sale) NEW"

 An R.O.S. form is an application for your new vehicle registration.

"R.O.S. (Report of Sale) USED"

An R.O.S. form reports the sale to the D.M.V. and serves as an application for registration for the used vehicle you are buying. Under certain circumstances you will be asked to sign a used car R.O.S. even though the car may be new. This may occur with what's known as an "unwind." This applies when a vehicle is sold then returned for one reason or another (financing unavailable, high payoff on trade, etc.) An R.O.S. NEW form can be filled out only once. Ask the dealer for a full explanation if you have been under the assumption you were buying a new car. If this is the case ask for a written "Statement of Facts." This explains in full the details of such circumstance. Be sure the dealer signs this form.

"STATEMENT OF FACTS"

The laws of disclosure in most states specify that if the vehicle has any special circumstances, the dealer must disclose them to you, such as "salvage title", "frame damage", "true mileage unknown", etc. Make sure you read and understand this form completely. DO NOT SIGN A BLANK FORM. Make sure it states what has been represented to you.

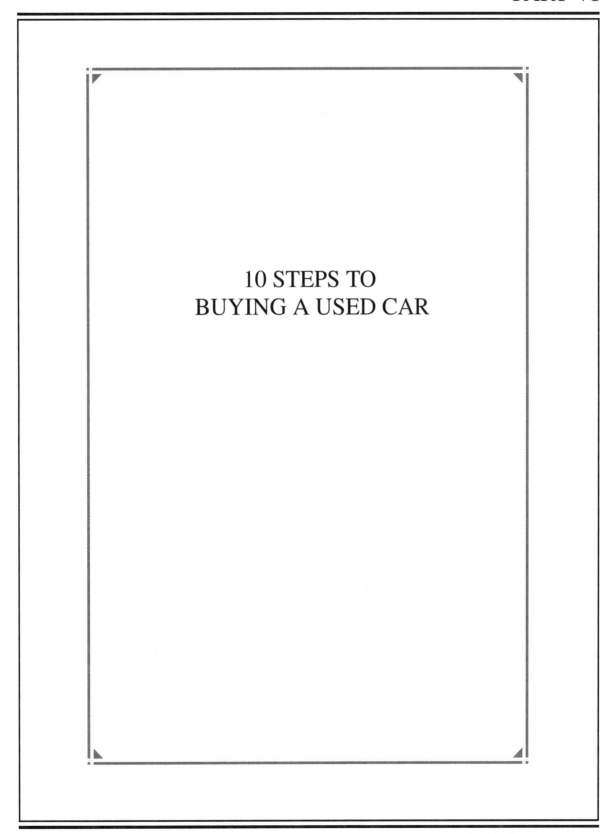

PART VI

10 STEPS TO
BUYING A USED CAR

10 Steps To Buying A Used Car:

1. VISUAL EXAMINATION:

A visual examination can give several quick clues as to the condition of the vehicle you are looking at. The body of the vehicle should appear smooth. The body joints should match up with each other. All the doors, as well as the hood and trunk should open and close with ease. Check for rust on the under body parts. Check for re-paint. Look at the tires. Check for uneven wear, tread, punctures holes, unusual bumps and ridges, etc.

Serious body damage may be checked for by having a mechanic put the car on a lift. Damage is indicated by weld marks, coil spring spacers or a bent frame. Check for oil or other fluid leaks. Examine the muffler, tail pipe and exhaust pipe for rust, soot, holes, oil, etc. which could indicate internal problems.

2. UNDER THE HOOD:

Check all hoses and belts for cracks and excess wear. Examine the battery for leaks and corrosion. Check the oil. Dark, dirty fluid could indicate that the car may not have been maintained properly. If the car is an automatic, check the transmission fluid. It should not be dark or have a burned odor to it.

3. ELECTRICAL SYSTEM:

Start the engine and check all accessories one at a time. Check gauges and instruments, radio, heater, air conditioner, windshield wipers and horn. Be sure to check all lights, including headlights, parking lights, turn signals, dome light, brake lights and warning lights on the dash. Also check the brake pedal for free play.

4. TRUNK:

Check the spare tire. If it is worn unevenly or is cupped (uneven bumps and ridges), something may be wrong with the front end. Be sure the vehicle has a jack and that it works.

5. SPRINGS AND SHOCKS:

Push down on the corners of the vehicle, front and back. It should not bounce up and down several times, since this indicates that the shock absorbers are worn. Stand back from the car and see if it sits level. If one corner is lower than another, one of the springs may be weak.

6. INTERIOR:

Badly worn carpeting, seats and upholstery can be a sign of heavy usage. If the seats have covers, look under them. Examine all safety belts.

7. THE ENGINE:

With the dealer's permission, race the engine a few quick bursts. Watch for excessive smoke out of the rear end. If a loud tapping noise occurs, have it checked out by a qualified mechanic.

A light tick or rapping in the top of the engine in not usually a serious problem, but a rapping noise may indicate a bad bearing. To check for a burnt valve or a tune-up problem, put the brakes on and drop it into drive. If the engine idles roughly, there may be a problem. To check for abnormal engine wear, put on the brakes and pull the PCV valve. If there is no heavy smoke or a small amount uniformly coming out, it's no problem. Heavy or puffing smoke indicates excessive wear.

8. DRIVE SHAFT AND REAR END:

If possible, take the car for a road test. Drive at approximately 35 miles per hour. Listen for rear end whines. If the car bounces or shakes, it's probably because the tires are unbalanced. If there is also an unpleasant droning, it could indicate a drive shaft or universal joint problem.

9. STEERING SYSTEM:

Drive on a straight road, holding the steering wheel lightly and check for play in the steering wheel. If the car pulls to the right or left, there is a problem. When rounding a corner, the steering wheel should turn smoothly and have a tendency to return smoothly to its straight ahead position.

10. BRAKES:

While driving 30 - 40 miles per hour, apply the brakes three or four times. If there is a pull to the left or right, there is a problem. Finally, slow down to about 5 miles per hour and brake lightly. Humping or an intermittent surge may indicate that the drums or rotors are out of round.

Major Defects That May Occur In A Used Vehicle:

Brake System:
Failure warning light broken
Pedal not firm under pressure
Not enough pedal reserve
Doesn't stop vehicle straight
Hoses damaged
Drum or rotor too thin
Lining or pad thickness less than 1/32 inch
Power unit not operating or leaking
Structural or mechanical parts damaged

Cooling System:
Leakage, including radiator
Waterpump not functioning properly

Differential:
Improper fluid level or leakage, excluding normal seepage
Visibly cracked or damaged housing
Abnormal noise or vibration caused by a faulty differential

Engine:
Abnormal oil leakage
Cracked block or head
Belts missing or inoperable
Knocks or misses related to camshaft
lifters and push rods

Electrical System:
Battery leakage
Alternator, generator, battery or starter functioning improperly

Exhaust System:
Leakage
Frame and Body
Frame-cracks, corrective welds
Rusted through Dogtracks
Bent or twisted frame

Fuel System:
Visible leakage
Inoperable Accessories
Gauges or warning devices
Air conditioner
Heater & Defroster

Steering System:
Too much free play at wheel
Free play in linkage more than 1/4 inch
Power unit fluid level improper
Steering gear binds or jams
Improperly aligned front wheels
Power unit belts cracked or slipping

Suspension System:
Ball joint seals damaged
Structural parts bent or damaged stabilizer bar disconnected
Spring broken
Shock absorber mounting loose
Rubber bushings damaged or missing
Radius rod damaged or missing
Shock absorber leaking or functioning improperly

Tires:
Tread depth less than 2/32 inches
Sizes mismatched
Visible damage

Wheels:
Visible cracks, damage or repairs
Mounting bolts loose or missing

PART VII

HOW TO SELL YOUR CAR

How To Sell Your Car:

Whether trading to a dealer or selling to a private party:

BODY:

Wash and wax your car and touch up small nicks and scratches. If major bodywork or repainting is required, determine whether you would do better by making the investment or by selling the car "as is."

INTERIOR:

Vacuum and dust. Cover worn carpeting with floor mats. If seats are torn or faded, purchase and install seat covers. Oil squeaky hinges and if necessary replace worn foot pedal pads.

ENGINE:

Remove oil and grease with products made for that purpose. Use a baking soda solution to clean the battery terminals. If it's needed, get a tune-up and then a Smog Check (this is now the seller's responsibility). While doing all of this may not get you a lot more for your car, it will definitely help you get the market value of your car.

WHAT PRICE SHOULD YOU ASK?:

Your best bet is to check the current Kelley blue or N.A.D.A. guide which can be found at your local library. Once you have found out both the wholesale and retail values compare these figures with the prices of comparable cars advertised in your local newspaper. By doing this you should have a pretty good idea of the price you can expect. It will normally be somewhere between the wholesale and retail values. Now determine your asking price as well as the minimum amount you would accept. Doing this, you are now ready to go to market with your car.

THE MARKET:

Your best bet is to advertise in your local newspaper on Friday, Saturday, and Sunday. This is when most people are looking to buy a car. In your advertisement use positive phrases like "one owner," "low mileage" or "excellent condition" if they truly apply.

SHOULD YOU STATE THE PRICE?:

There is a debate about the wisdom of stating your price. We suggest that you do include the price in your ad. By doing so you will eliminate people looking for give-a-ways. But when stating your price always suggest negotiability (i.e. asking $4,600.00 or $4,600.00 O.B.O.)

CAUTION:

Most people will want to road test your car and perhaps have a mechanic inspect it. However, be wary of car thieves and irresponsible drivers. Always join the prospective buyer on the test drive. If that's not possible, protect yourself by asking to see their driver's license and one other form of identification. Record the information. Agree to a reasonable amount of time for the excursion, but no more than one hour. It is always best if the person arrives by car and leaves that car while testing yours....but once again, be careful to get identification. The car they came in may have been stolen.

PAYMENT:

Accept only cash or a certified check made out to you. If it is a personal check go with the buyer to their bank to have it cashed. DO NOT transfer title until you have been fully paid.

NOTIFICATION:

Let the D.M.V. know of the sale so that you won't be held responsible for the new owner traffic violations, parking citations, or civil and criminal activities. Also notify your insurance company.

As we stated earlier, the Smog Certificate is now the seller's responsibility. The following information will help you in obtaining one.

PART VIII

HOW TO GET A SMOG CHECK

How To Get A Smog Check:

Just follow the few easy steps listed below to get your Smog Check inspection. When you are due to have a Smog Check test -- required every two years in specially designated areas -- a notice will be printed on the vehicle registration renewal form you receive from the Department of Motor Vehicles (DMV).

After you receive your notice:

1. Drive to the official Smog Check inspection station of your choice - a garage, service station or dealership displaying the familiar Smog Check sign.

2. After completing a three-part test which includes a visual exam, a functional check and a computerized tailpipe emissions measurement, your mechanic will provide you with the test results.

If your vehicle passes you will be issued a Smog Check certificate. If your vehicle fails, you are not required to spend more than the amount shown on the chart below to pass a second Smog Check inspection.

VEHICLE AGE	LIMIT
1971 & Older	50.00
1972- 74	90.00
1975 - 79	125.00
1980 -89	175.00
1990 & Newer	300.00

3. After receiving your Smog Check certificate, retain it for the buyer as they will need it to transfer it to their name.

SOME CHANGES

Recent changes in the Smog Check laws include: 1966 and newer model gasoline powered passenger cars and light trucks up to 8,500 pounds gross vehicle weight in the program. In addition, the law now requires the SELLER in private party transactions to provide the buyer with a smog certificate prior to or at the time of vehicle transfer.

Also, effective January 1, 1990, heavy-duty vehicles (8,501 pounds gross vehicle weight and over, including commercial and recreational vehicles), will be subject to the program. All liquid-propane gas (LPG), natural gas (LNG/CNG) and methanol-powered vehicles registered in the program areas are also included. At the same time, auto manufacturers must provide a three (3) year/50,000 mile emissions control warranty and a seven (7) year/70,000 mile warranty to cover replacement of emissions control parts costing more than $300.00 on all 1990 and newer vehicles.

If You Need Repairs:

1. The law requires that you receive a written estimate before the work is done and an invoice after the work is completed.

2. Feel free to shop around for the best inspection and repair prices. If your vehicle fails its Smog Check, many stations will re-inspect it free of charge if you hire them to make the repairs. While the Bureau of Automotive Repair (BAR) does not regulate inspection fees, the Smog Check certificate is $7.00.

3. If you fail re-inspection after the Smog Check repairs are made, you have the right to take your vehicle to a referee station. A referee may issue a certificate if the repairs were made within the cost limit but were not sufficient for your vehicle to pass the Smog Check test. Ask your Smog Check mechanic for a referral to the referee station nearest you. However, vehicles under warranty are required to have any warranty covered defects corrected before a certificate or waiver can be issued.

What Is B.A.R.?:

The Bureau of Automotive Repair is a consumer protection agency that administers and enforces the California Smog Check Program. BAR can issue citations to mechanics who fail to repair vehicles in accordance with bureau-established repair procedures, as well as to stations that fail to provide estimates and invoices. If you have a dispute that you cannot resolve with an auto repair dealer, you may request assistance from BAR by contacting the BAR office nearest you.

PART IX

SMOG REFEREE PROCESS

Smog Referee Process:

(What to do when your car can't pass its Smog Check)

WHAT IS A REFEREE?

A referee is a privately run testing facility under contract with the Bureau of Automotive Repair (BAR). The referee assists motorists who are unable to obtain a smog certificate from a licensed Smog Check station.

WHO IS ELIGIBLE FOR REFEREE ASSISTANCE?

Motorists are eligible for help from a referee under various conditions including the following:

1. Your vehicle failed and you think it was improperly tested and/or repaired at a licensed Smog Check station.
2. Repairs up to the cost limit will not reduce tailpipe emissions.
3. Your vehicle is exempt, but you received a DMV renewal notice stamped "Smog Check required."
4. Your engine is replaced with an engine not originally equipped for that year, make or model vehicle.
5. You have a non-conforming vehicle, i.e. grey market, kit car, etc.
6. You want verification of your vehicle's emission control warranty.
7. A missing emission control part is not available.
8. You need a replacement certificate.

WHAT CAN THE REFEREE DO FOR ME?

DISPUTE RESOLUTION

If you think your vehicle was improperly tested and/or failed by a licensed Smog Check station, make an appointment with the referee. Be sure to take a copy of the station's invoice, and the vehicle inspection report with you.

The referee will re-inspect your vehicle and will issue a certificate if it passes the inspection.

COST LIMIT

If your vehicle failed the tailpipe emissions test and the Smog Check station determines there are no missing, modified or disconnected emission control devices and:

1. Repairs up to the cost limit will not reduce tailpipe emissions.
2. Repairs and/or adjustments have been made up to the cost

limit, and the vehicle still fails, then the referee will issue a certificate.

EXEMPTIONS

If your vehicle is exempt from Smog Check, (diesel, electric powered vehicles, or a two-cycle engine or engine under 50 cubic inch displacement) but your registration renewal form says "Smog Check required," the referee will verify the exemption and issue a smog certificate.

ENGINE REPLACEMENTS

This applies when the original engine has been removed and replaced with an engine not originally equipped for that year, make or model vehicle. Your Smog Check station can help identify an engine change during an inspection. Make an appointment with the referee and bring all available bills, receipts, etc. with you. The referee will verify the engine change, and either issue a certificate and attach a BAR label or advise you of further requirements. Once the referee attaches a BAR label, the vehicle can be tested at any Smog Check station.

GREY MARKET VEHICLES

Grey market vehicles are vehicles that have been directly imported to California and do not meet California, US or EPA standards. Smog Check stations should not initially inspect these vehicles. Make an appointment with the referee and bring a copy of the EPA test report to the appointment. The referee will inspect your vehicle and attach a BAR label to the door post if the vehicle meets the BAR criteria. Once a BAR label is attached, the vehicle can be tested at any Smog Check station.

KIT CARS

If you own a specially constructed vehicle like a dune buggy, kit car or antique vehicle, make an appointment with the referee. Take any bills, receipts or written statements from an auto repair shop verifying the year, make and model of engine and chassis. If the vehicle meets BAR criteria, the referee will attach a BAR label. Once a BAR label is attached, the vehicle can be tested at any Smog Check station.

WARRANTY DISPUTES

If your vehicle's emission control system is covered under warranty, and you have a dispute with the Smog Check station, make an appointment with the referee for verification.

PARTS EXEMPTION

If your vehicle has failed the inspection due to missing emission control system parts and your Smog Check station cannot locate the part(s), contact the Parts Locator/Exemption toll-free line at (800) 826-3566. If the part cannot be located, you will be issued a "limited parts exemption." After you receive the exemption, make an appointment with the referee (be sure to take the exemption slip with you).

This process must be repeated every time a smog inspection is required.

REPLACEMENT CERTIFICATES

If your smog certificate has been lost or stolen and you still have your vehicle inspection report, make an appointment with the referee. The referee will inspect your vehicle and if it passes, will issue another certificate for $6.00

This must be done within 90 days of the original inspection.

FOR A REFEREE NEAR YOU CALL
1-800-622-7733

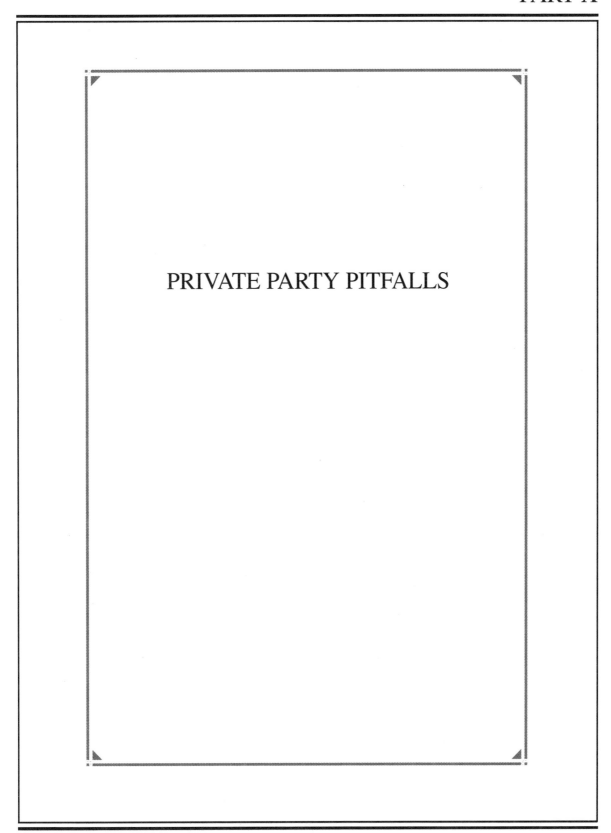

PART X

PRIVATE PARTY PITFALLS

Private Party Pitfalls:

Below is list of problems that could occur when buying "private party:"

1. YOU COULD BE ROBBED:

Criminals wait in parking lots with "for sale" signs on their car insisting on cash payment. When the money is revealed, the subject is robbed. End result....no money....no car.

2. STOLEN CAR:

The car is stolen. There are many ways for thieves to sell stolen cars. Sometimes they have stolen the title also. End result....no money....no car.

3. UNSAFE VEHICLES:

Who in their right mind would buy an unsafe vehicle? It is against the law for a "Dealer" to sell an unsafe vehicle. There is no law to cover a "private party" transaction. Unsafe vehicles could be:
A. Salvage vehicles
B. Flood cars
C. Taxis
D. Salvage-like vehicles that were in major accidents and pieced back together. These types of cars must be avoided all together. No one should risk their life for a couple of hundred bucks! (See Dealer required safety items.)

4. SMOG CERTIFICATES:

Often cars are sold without smog certificates. Buying a car without a smog certificate is foolish. Problems range from cars which cannot be registered, costing hundreds, even thousands to bring into compliance. Beware of counterfeit certificates. They make great wallpaper, but aren't accepted at the D.M.V.

5. VEHICLES WITH EXISTING LIENS:

The presence of a lien holder is not always obvious, especially those originating from states other than California. Not even the absence of one on the title is 100% reliable. If there is a lien holder with money owed on the vehicle, the lien holder owns the vehicle until they are paid in full.

6. NO TITLE - LOST TITLE - DUPLICATE OR INVALID TITLES:

A person cannot transfer ownership of a motor vehicle without a valid title. Know who you're dealing with. Why pay good money for something you can't own?

7. BOGUS YEAR STICKER:

Along with your registration, you are given the corresponding year's sticker. To get around the cost of registration, some folks just take one from another vehicle. This could cost you hundreds for each year they cheated.

8. ODOMETER DISCREPANCY:

There is a Federal law against tampering with the odometer. This still doesn't stop the crooks. If you don't complain or have evidence, who's to know? Buyer Beware!

9. WARRANTY:

Have you ever heard of "private parties" offering a warranty? Even if they did, how could you enforce the agreement? Buy from a licensed dealer.

10. PARKING TICKETS:

Parking violations are posted against the vehicle, not the driver. It is not unusual for a vehicle to have thousands of dollars in parking tickets. Check before you buy.

Example: You purchase a vehicle from a nice couple. They have a nice home, identification and the proper documents. At the D.M.V. you are told to pay an additional $1800.00 for traffic outstanding violations against the car.

11. ACCIDENTS:

Would you like to buy a vehicle that was recently in a "hit and run" accident? How do you know?

12. WARRANTY RETURNS:
Terms like "warranty return," "rebuilt," or "salvage." If these are present on a title, they seriously reduce the value of a vehicle. A dealer must disclose these conditions to you in writing. The public is under no such obligation.

13. UNRECORDED TRANSFERS:

Each time a vehicle is sold, it is considered a transfer whether or not it is completed at the D.M.V. The subsequent purchaser is liable for the costs incurred by all previous owners.

14. LOW PRICE MISCONCEPTIONS:

Some believe that prices are lower in the private sector. More often than not, the purchaser is lulled into paying more by believing this to be true.

15. MECHANIC'S INSPECTION:

By law, a dealer must let you have a vehicle that you are considering purchasing inspected by a mechanic. The guy on the street corner is under no such obligation to comply.

16. N.S.F. CHECK TO THE D.M.V.:

The D.M.V. will issue documents accepting a check as payment. If the check is not honored at the bank, the documents are invalid. The subsequent purchaser must pay all fees and penalties due against the vehicle.

17. OUT OF STATE VEHICLES:

Just by virtue of being from another state does not make a vehicle undesirable. Unfortunately, the state of California charges an extra $300.00 for the introduction of an out of state vehicle. The titling documents vary from state to state, even professionals are sometimes confused.

18. TAX AND LICENSE:

Most people don't realize that when they go to the D.M.V. to register a used car bought from a private party, they must pay sales tax and license in full, right then.

Private Party Safety Test:

As stated in the "Private Party Pitfalls" section, I do not recommend purchasing private party vehicles unless you know the seller personally and the vehicle's history. If you decide to venture into the private party market, use the following test to validate the car. If the answer is "no" to any question, there may be an unknown possible liability.

Question 1. Does the Vehicle I.D. number match the registration documents?

Question 2. Is the person selling the vehicle the registered owner?

Question 3. Is the seller willing to show you identification as well as give you their home address and phone number?

Question 4. Is the vehicle certified for sale in California or the U.S. and not an imported non-conforming vehicle?

Question 5. Are all emission control components installed and functioning as listed on the under-hood label?

Question 6. Does the seller have a current smog certificate and all legal documentation required to transfer the vehicle to your name?

Question 7. Is the vehicle's title (pink slip) free of words such as "salvage," "police," "warranty re-turn?"

Question 8. Is the vehicle free of all liens and encumbrances including parking tickets?

Question 9. Does the year sticker on the license plate match the expiration date of their most current registration?

Question 10. Does the odometer work and appear to be tamper free?

Question 11. Are you confident the vehicle has never been in an accident and has never had any major collision repair work?

Question 12. Is the prospective seller willing to allow you to have the vehicle checked out by a certified mechanic?

Question 13. Is this car currently registered?

PART XI

DEALER RESPONSIBILITIES

Dealer Responsibilities:

When buying a used vehicle, most consumer advocates recommend purchasing from a licensed dealer, primarily because by virtue of their license you (the buyer) become automatically entitled to numerous rights which do not apply when buying from a private party. Unfortunately, there are no comprehensive regulations protecting consumers who choose to purchase an automobile in the private party market.

In this section we have tried to address some of the most common concerns of the consumer regarding the buyer's rights and the licensed dealer. If you have any problems or questions regarding your rights after you purchase, your best bet is to contact your local D.M.V.

The D.M.V. is the agency that oversees the licensing of legitimate auto dealers and will assist in directing you to the right individual or agency to help resolve the matter.

Should you have a legitimate complaint concerning the transaction of the vehicle, we recommend you contact the Sales Manager or General Manager of the dealership who sold you the car. You should discuss the problem or complaint with this person. If the dealership is legitimate, most complaints will be resolved to your satisfaction. A licensed dealer realizes to stay in business for any length of time they must do two things...comply with the laws that regulate their license and keep their customers happy. The laws that regulate licensed dealers can be found in the State Vehicle Code which is available at any D.M.V. office at a very reasonable cost (less than $5.00).

The most common question most people have regarding the dealer is their responsibilities prior to sale. These are commonly referred to as "Safety Items." The following page lists the most common items required by the dealer as stated in Division 12 of the Vehicle Code. The law states that it is "unlawful for a dealer to sell any unsafe vehicle."

Dealer "Safety Items":

The following items must be installed and operable at the time of sale.

LIGHTS:

All lights must operate at a minimum of 85% of designed voltage.

- Headlamps (min. 2) including proper alignment
- Turn Signals (front and rear)
- Dimmer Switch (High/Low Beams)
- Back-up Lights

MECHANICAL:

- Brakes (all components)
- Tires (minimum 1/32 " of tread)
- Battery

MISCELLANEOUS:

- Horn
- Rear View Mirror
- Safety Belts (all seats)
- Windshield (cracks/pits)
- Windshield Defroster
- License Plate Light
- Stop Lights
- High Beam Indicator
- Tail Lamps
- Struts/Shocks
- Smog Equipment
- Wipers (2)
- Windshield Defroster
- Speedometer/Odometer
- Rear Windows (unimpaired)

THE DEALER MUST ALSO REPAIR ALL UNLAWFUL EQUIPMENT WHICH INCLUDES:

- Under or Over Sized Steering Wheel
- Noise Standards (Exhaust System)
- Vehicle Height (raised or lowered over legal limits)
- Recapped Tires
- Tinted Glass (film)

Use The Book:

Throughout this book we have tried to give you an inside look at all aspects of the automotive industry. Hopefully, this information will help you avoid the aggravation usually associated with purchasing an automobile. We suggest you reference this material everytime you intend to enter into an automotive transaction.

In the back of the book you will find a couple of note pages. Use them to record pertinent information regarding your upcoming automobile purchase. Have your notes and the book handy when entering the dealership. It will have a profound psychological effect on the individuals you will be dealing with. Even with this edge, there is no replacement for common sense. Remember, your very best tactic as a buyer is remembering that you are the paying customer and have the right to be treated as such. Good luck and God Bless.

NOTES

NOTES